Henry Beissel's Previous Books of Poetry & Plays

Poetry

Witness the Heart
New Wings for Icarus
Race on the Dark
The Salt I Taste
Cantos North
Season of Blood
Poems New and Selected
Ammonite
Stones to Harvest
Dying I was Born
The Dragon and the Pearl
The Price of Morning (Walter Bauer)
A Different Sun (Walter Bauer)
A Thistle in His Mouth (Peter Huchel)
Letters on Birchbark (Uta Regoli)

Plays

Inuk and the Sun
Goya
Under Coyote's Eye
The Noose
Improvisations for Mr. X
For Crying Out Loud
The Apple Orchard (Walter Bauer)
The Curve (Tankred Dorst)
A Trumpet for Nap (Tankred Dorst)
Waiting for Gaudreault (André Simard; co-translator: Arlette Francière
Are You Afraid of Thieves? (Louis-Dominique Lavigne)
The Emigrants (Slawomir Mrozek)
Hedda Gabler (Henrik Ibsen)
All Corpses Are Equal (Shie Min; co-translator Jia-Lin Peng)
Sacrifices (Shie Min; con-translator Jia-Lin Peng)
The Glass Mountain (Tor Åge Bringsvaerd; co-translator Per Brask)

Across the Sun's Warp

Across the Sun's Warp

a poem

by

Henry Beissel

BuschekBooks

National Library of Canada Cataloguing in Publication Data

Beissel, Henry, 1929-
    Across the sun's warp / by Henry Beissel.

Poems.
ISBN 1-894543-16-5

    I. Title.

PS8565.A6656D745 2003   C811'.6   C2003-904801-2

Printed in Canada by Hignell Book Printing, Winnipeg, Manitoba.

BuschekBooks gratefully acknowledges the support of the Canada Council for the Arts and the Ontario Arts Council for its publishing program.

BuschekBooks
P.O. Box 74053, 5 Beechwood Avenue
Ottawa, Ontario K1M 2H9
Canada
Email: buschek.books@sympatico.ca

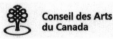

**Conseil des Arts
du Canada**   **Canada Council
for the Arts**

ONTARIO ARTS COUNCIL
CONSEIL DES ARTS DE L'ONTARIO

When I regard all the world
As my brother
Why is it that its tranquillity
Should be so thoughtlessly disturbed?
Sublime is the moment
When the world is at peace.

Emperor Hirohito

Dawn has emerged from a thunderstorm
to the tune of birds rejoicing in the wind
and the tonic rain. Leaf by leaf the light
lowers itself from treetops slides down
the rain's steaming pathways and ignites
green flames we call forests and meadows.
From the thin watercolour hues of dawn
a single hour transmutes the sky into liquid
gold and azure so luminous it seeps into
the crampest of rock crevices, spills into
rodents' burrows in the fields and in cities
splashes around blinds still drawn, flows
soundless under closed doors and bursts
through myriads of windows boisterous
to flood the dark sequestered spaces
we call home—
                    but with light comes heat
and heat draws veils of vapour from lakes
and rivers, obscures what's here and now
weighs the mind down with flickering
images of a horror movie: Hiroshima,
mon amour, where seven rivers float
this same morning radiantly down
to Sento Bay into aquamarine lucence.

                    August is the month Confucius
                    was born who knew to love truth
                          is better than to know it—
                    and the Mayflower set sail from
                          Southampton with the truth
                    of winds and seas to carry the seeds
                    of a new nation and a millennial creed
                    across the ocean: one-hundred-and-two
                    pilgrims who never knew they would
                    launch that same month centuries apart
                          the Klondike Goldrush, Voyager 2
                          beyond Jupiter and Saturn,
                          and from Tinian Island
                          the *Enola Gay* to Hiroshima.

                          Thus do fancy and folly
                          sit in each other's lap
                          and conceive absurdities

while the sun soars through the lion's constellation
shaking its golden mane as it travels at 240 km/sec
230 million years to round the galaxy once, radiating
2×10^{36} ergs/min into a vast silence to light up
the solitary planets, give warmth here to grasslands
and oceans, wings to birds and insects,
energy to lovers to pump new life into clouds
and stones that will in time reclaim them.

On time's loom nature
Threads stones across the sun's warp
To weave a garden
As clouds shuttle the seasons
And stretch life from birth to death.

Day by day the tilted axis of the world
is spinning night now north of the equator
toward the equinox that must return to darkness
the dominion it maintains throughout the universe.
The sun's shadow unveils the cosmic landscape
for all its sparkling emptiness, its black hostility
to us, to life, even as summer nights take
the luminous pulse of fireflies signalling their passion
to their mates and the low rumble of thunder
promises rain. Sultry midsummer storms drum dawn
into consciousness, the light leaden, the rain black
pearls cascading down the roof, washing memories
heavy with the crude of nightmares to the shores
of awareness, polluting what's familiar, menacing
what's lovable in our green ignorance
till the morning begins to devour the shadows.

It's 8 o'clock. August 6.
This day half a century or so ago
and half a spin of the globe away
the U.S.A. made history a tale
of horror only the most reasonable
of monsters could've invented:
The Force from which the Sun Draws its Power
Unleashed
against children on their way

to school or in the classroom
their eyes full of sunshine
curiosity mischief...against
student work brigades
of boys and girls assembling
in the city's streets and squares...
against doctors teachers nurses—
civilians young and old, sleeping
waking unsuspecting unarmed...
The Greatest Achievement of Science
unleashed!

Rutherford unravelled the radioactive
disintegration of uranium into α and β rays
at the turn of this blood-soaked century
and left us nowhere to hide from a radiance
turned into radiation. He bombarded nitrogen
with energetic radium forcing a proton
from the nucleus to make the alchemists' dream
come true: the transmutation of elements.
Boron into nitrogen into oxygen,
aluminum into phosphorus into silicon—
the atom was split! But the philosopher's stone
Noah hung in the ark to give light
to every creature was found to be
more lethal than a samurai sword.

It must have begun in time immemorial.
Two gods on the floating bridge of heaven
dipped their star-studded spears in the ocean
and created the land of the rising sun. Something
stirred between the clouds and the stones.
Water engendered a genesis both random
and prefigured, a garden rose from the sea
whose freedom inspired cells to arrange
and rearrange themselves in a pattern of mind.
Laboriously, by trial and error, indifferent
to its victims, life wrote its codes of survival
into law as continents moved and seasons
shifted. Against all the odds of climate and
cataclysm the children of the sun spread

till *homo sapiens* reached all the world's coasts.
When the last ice melted, the rising waters
left 3,300 islands stranded in the Pacific and
its inhabitants free to struggle with their own
demons on the narrow road to insight.

We have walked
the eightfold way
of the subatomic world
and found every particle
has its anti-particle, every
electron its positron
and when they meet
in their contrariness
they annihilate each other
vanishing in a flash
of energy 90 trillion times
their mass, leaving
γ rays that destroy
living cells. Einstein
showed the way
but couldn't tell why
all things being equal
when the yes met the no
forces in the primal
clash a dozen or so
billion years ago
why anything at all
was left over
to constitute matter:
any electrons muons taus
and their neutrinos
any baryons mesons
or their quarks
from which to make
the stars and stones, rivers
fish, flesh and the mind
that wants to know.
The mystery of matter is
itself a question of survival.

How blue and tranquil the sky.
The fussy drone of a bumblebee
more obtrusive than the hum
of a single B-29 superfortress.
There was a war somewhere
all but forgotten in this radiant
dawn and the sirens had sounded
the all-clear. What more
could the heart desire
from a summer's day?
But the morning came up
with a big surprise—the biggest
and bloodiest deception since Troy
was devastated by a horse.

Hahn and Fermi fired neutrons at 15,000 km/sec
like bullets to penetrate the atom's nucleus.
Like gods they created new elements. Uranium
yielded plutonium fissioned into transuranian
unstable elements as neutrons set free fresh neutrons
that freed more neutrons in a resonance process
that triggered a chain reaction that released enough
energy to meet all our needs and fancies on this planet
unto its fiery death. $E=mc^2$ where c is the speed
with which the sun lights and powers the planets
and the spaces between them, the stones and the clouds,
our flora and fauna, you and me. But the power
proved too much and the light too little for us.
Sicut eritis dei—motto of the blind leading the blind!

What the eye sees and the hand touches
is a construct of the mind, no more,
no less. The eye can scan a seashore
and watch the water shatter in the surf
but it cannot see the architecture in a single
drop or the scheme of molecules in a wave
tenuous and tenacious as a thought. The hand
against the maple trunk can sense the surging
sap, but it cannot feel the turmoil in the tree's
atomic pith any more than the foot can apprehend
the fiery furor at the earth's core. We walk
between dimensions too vast and too minute
for us to encompass though they encompass us.

The frenzy of elementary particles is as invisible
to us as the four forces that contain them,
that forever explode and reassemble stars.
What the laughing philosopher thought to be
eternal and indivisible turned out a mad
composition for dancing figures of energy
that made men of reason into monsters figuring
that a kilo of uranium-235 or plutonium-239
could be rigged inside a container to trigger
an explosion that would erase a city in seconds
and incinerate its population, perhaps even
set off a chain reaction that would turn earth
into a supernova fireball. Prometheus' powers
in the hands of madmen. Oppie and his gang
knew the risks but they could only guess
at the reality, and so they built the bomb,
unleashed a force to produce *The Greatest
Simultaneous Slaughter in the Whole History
of Mankind*, turning Hollywood dreams into
a nightmare from which we have yet to awaken.

Stand by for the tone break—and the turn:
the final words of the pre-nuclear age precisely at 8:15:17 a.m.
the greatest achievement of science weighing 9,000 pounds and 30,800 feet high
dropped precisely from a blue tranquil summer sky headed for the T-shaped Aioi bridge
over the Ota river at Long.132º 23' 29" E Lat. 34º 23' 29" N exploded precisely as planned
43 secs later well not quite as precisely perhaps the wind or the instruments or the bomber's
hand trembled for *Little Boy* missed by 800 ft and detonated above Shima Hospital whose staff
and patients were instantly precisely vaporized along with a hundred thousand civilians approx
incinerated by the forces from which the sun draws its power across the warped minds of men
in faraway Potsdam Harry formally announced the event
I've never felt happier in my life
and Joe was furious
for having been
bested mind set
on executions
back home and
Winston gloating
over Moscow's
upset over the
Hiroshima roast
half the city's
population torched
the rest rotting
slowly to ashes
under a charred
radioactive
sky charred
radioactive
children
Little Boy had spoken
and the world ended as it had begun with a big bang and a flash

A thunderstorm may clear the air
but it cannot wipe clean the slate
the poet has covered with question
and exclamation marks measuring
the inwit of our kind. The sun
pulls itself up over the horizon
on a dark fury of clouds and inspires
the morning with voices near and far.
The robin trades dulcet phrases
with the light, the chickadees chatter
with the rain that still drips languidly
from leaf to leaf, the imperious bluejays
call their little world stridently to order
and attention—echoes of the chirping
warbling piping whistling musical riot
that greeted us before we could name it
and has accompanied us ever since.
We've come a long way from Africa
since the forests withdrew from us
and we lumbered into the savannah
where we learnt to walk with the sun
and the rains across every continent
to tame oxen and horses, grasses
and trees, which in turn tamed us,
forced us to serve them and build
huts houses villages towns cities
where the tumult of machines
has long made the birds inaudible.

Two fawns break from underbrush
high as hay around my den
flushed by the pressing green
from a jumble of raspberry bushes
ferns goldenrod boneset elecampane
nettles grasses and countless seedlings
of ash cedar elm hemlock and maple.
Their spotted cinnamon fur is
as startling as the sinewed grace
of their movements—abruptly, at short
intervals, their heads jerk erect and
they stand, one leg arrested in mid-air,

stock-still, in mid-motion, intent
on catching a scent, a sign,
the hazel chatoyancy of their eyes
bulging with the strain to see
the unseen, their ears extended
to scoop from the stream of sound
the tiniest atom of danger.
In the heart of such stillness we know
we share the fragility the mystery
and the mind reaches out gives
itself up to an impossible embrace
beyond the indignities and hostilities
survival forces on us. The frisky fawns
leap back into the green waves
of their element at the slightest
smell sound or sight of me.

What if the deer know
We are no longer at home
Here where we belong
Among the grasses and trees
Home is always a journey.

Hunter-gatherers roamed the islands
of Japan ten thousand years ago
not only in pursuit of fish and flesh,
root and fruit, but on a quest
that took them from pottery to poetry
when they settled down to grow rice
in the warm moist winds blowing
from the sea. As the planet warmed
their hearts warmed to its beauty
and they saw patterns in the caves
of their skulls, brought them outside
and played with them in the light
till they captured something
of the spirit of the rivers on whose banks
they camped and of the mountains
which were sacred, something they felt
but couldn't say except in the play
of lines and shapes in low relief

17

the Jōmon people indulged
with baroque intricacy on their pots
and later the Yayori tamed
in simpler designs to adorn
the vessels that held wine and water.
Thus they learnt to speak to their gods.
They etched patterns of beauty
into iron and bronze from which they learnt
to make tools—and weapons
for with settlement came possessions
and with possessions war.

Bronze bells call for peace
But peasants with iron swords
Face in bronze mirrors
Samurai planting rice and
Harvesting only corpses.

August 6, 1945, Colonel Tibbets flew a mission
that bore his mother's name: Enola Gay.
He handpicked the B-29 to drop the A-bomb
assembled in sight of the Sangre de Cristo
mountain range at Los Alamos by a crew
of miracle workers with no more scruples
than the chalk they used to scrawl the math
of their inferno on blackboards, no more compassion
than the medical doctors in Dachau conducting
deep-freeze research on prisoners screaming
behind glass walls, or the professors from Kyoto
National University at Unit 731 in Manchuria
infecting POWs with bubonic plague, syphilis
and hemorrhagic fever and dissecting them
still alive to test bacteriological weapons.
In New Mexico they had different names:
like the chutzpa Teller, pusher and puffer
of the bomb (who estimated the risk of blowing up
the planet three in a million and therefore reasonable),
or the sleazy Szilard, too lazy to flush the toilet
(*That's what maids are for!*) but frantic to see the bomb
dropped and collect $750,000 for inventing it—
that's about $2 per head of child woman and man

killed by the bomb (if you include Nagasaki).
Better dead than red—or was it yellow?
Scientists are no more colour-blind than politicians,
and we all know about slit-eyes. *The Japs*, the President
explained, *are beasts and have to be treated as beasts.*
Would Harry vaporize, incinerate or merely flense
the two fawns who prudently slipped back into the fragile
safety of the forest which shelters my home and my mind?

Give me the light
of compassion to show
the trail between fear
and greed. Give us
the feel of the wind
and the taste of rain
for a communion
with all that lives.
The petals of every flower
extract from the sun
a colour to love
and every bird balances
the universe on the tip
of its wings. The blue
jays are brighter
than our ideas
and dawn is true.

Is the model we have made of matter more true?
Six leptons and six quarks subjected
to four forces mediated by eight gluons,
two W particles, the Z^o, and the photon.
But what mediates the attraction between
the Milky Way and the Andromeda Galaxy,
the sun and the earth, between you and me?
Let me hold your hand and look in your eyes:
a photon is as weightless as a kiss but
in the world we inhabit love is stronger
than the force between quarks and gluons.
Particles pop into and out of existence from nothing
in fractions of microseconds and you cannot know
where they are if you measure their speed

but in each other's arms we are the embrace
where the universe finds temporary peace.
The three-coloured quarks have no colour
and their flavours are without taste. Perhaps
the strange charms of their up and down bottoms
and tops are strategies of the cosmos to cuckold
reason.—Three cheers for Mark in Isolde's quark!

Sunflowers shake their heads
in the hot wind that ruffles
the floral plumes of goldenrod.
Briskly hummingbirds zoom
among diminishing flowers.
Like soft purring helicopters
they hover over petal lips
to refuel sweetness and light
with the swiftest of tongue thrusts.
Underground tumescent roots
suck the soil while blueberries
are ripening in the sun and apples
strain the elegance of branches
against another fall. Every hour
creeps closer to the gathering
dark and we must take sides
with the scattered forces of light
to find a way home to the future.

The brain questing must
Cross its bridges in darkness
Clouds and trees are black
At night even in moonlight
Bats listen to what they seek.

It is still August 6, 1945—
a date not carved but blasted
forever into the rock of the ages
by an explosion with the force of more
than 12 kilotons of TNT—the full load
of 3,000 B-29 flying fortresses
packed into a single plane
into a single the first atomic bomb.

It was Hitler who promised:
Wir werden ihre Städte ausradieren,
but a B-29 made good on it.

At 8:16:00 hours precisely—the bomb's metal casing
seared into ionized gas—1.5 milliseconds later a flash
as hot as the sun's interior (fifty million degrees)—
from heaven fell the fires of hell—a fireball appeared
above Shima Hospital—for an instant the glory of light
absolute as it was in the beginning—exploded expanded
burst into a firestorm—a giant 300,000° C flame flicked
once across the stunned city, licked streets and buildings
clean of everything alive, everything moving or movable—
licked the city clean of buildings and streets—leaving
within 10 seconds a 132 km² smouldering wasteland—
thousands witnessed the fire in the forge of stars were
turned to ashes and rose into the sky—their pain
and their perplexity never caught up with them—the sun's
warp blasted them into the void of eternity—they became
the last blinding image on their retina melting instantly
evaporating—a whitehot blank—nothing but ashes ashes
ashes billowing—you can no longer tell woman from man,
horse from dog, door from shrine from roof in a cloud
of ashes—for all flesh is as the grass is ash and stone is
ash and ash is as—a thick cloud raining black death
on the unlucky survivors—lucky the ones who were
vaporized instantly—never to know the lingering torture
of dying radioactively—not to know what might have been
nor what happened retroactively—nor what was had been...

Luck is as capricious as the light:
both withhold, bestow or withdraw
their favours by happenstance alone.
Outside my window three comfrey
plants hold their white corybs
high into the August sun.
A foot further east on my path
they would not have survived
the mower past first greening.
By the edge of the pond a heron
sits rigid long enough for a frog

to jump too soon. You, my lucky
reader, and I, your voice, share
our good fortune to be here
now watching the light luxuriate
in a plethora of leaves outside,
then listening to the music of words
as we pursue signs and pointers
on the page promising to bring us
to our senses or our senses to us:
the smell of mint in the garden,
a melody on a violin, the touch
of your lover's hair, the taste
of salt on a seabreeze, the painter's
brush conjuring energy in colour—
but for a different roll of fate's dice
we would have none of it, or we might
have been the melody, the seabreeze,
the brush, or we might have found
ourselves in the hell of Hiroshima—

a city born four centuries ago in the shadow
of a castle the *damyo* of the Mori clan built
by the mouth of the Ōta river. All our cities
were built from fear and greed. Peasants,
artisans, soldiers, priests, and stewards
have always flocked to the walls of forts
and castles, their numbers growing in proportion
to the appetite for power and possessions
of the lords and masters who needed them
as much as they needed their protection. Fateful
symbiosis where blood must flow for peace to reign.

In the beginning the emperor was born
to the goddess of the sun. That's how
Jimmu entered *kami*—apotheosis of all
things majestic extraordinary mysterious:
rivers and mountains, grasses and trees,
the ocean and the sky, the beasts on land
in the sea and in the air. His appointment
was divine: to guide his people *kami*
no michi—in the ways of the gods

to cleanse themselves of pollution
from death and disease, of the stains
of selfish actions, and to build shrines
festooning *torii* and sacred trees
with ropes of straw flying
their prayers on strips of paper to express
their hopes for a good harvest and
their gratitude when it was brought in.
And the Shinto gods were good to Yamamoto
people who danced for the sun goddess
and decorated their majestic burial mounds
with *haniwa* cylinders of rufous-brown clay.

> On the spirit's path
> All that exists is sacred
> Clouds stones and trees talk
> Of the golden sun dancing
> Singing the whole world night long.

The light is now dancing
between bush and tree
from flower to leaf
and across the pond
like a swarm of brimstone
butterflies. The dizzy
velocities of photons
are invisible, resolved
in the greens and yellows
and the blue of a still-life
of heaven and earth
the morning has stretched
across my window.
A covey of ruffed grouse
crosses my footpath
in slow staccato
motion without disturbing
this calm world.
Only my words
come upon its serenity
like a blustering wind
ruffling tranquil

                                        waters. Naming it
                            we wrench the unnameable
                             out of shape out of place
                                   we pass judgment
                                  where all is equal.
                                    To speak is to be
                                 human. We inherited
                                  an unnatural order
                               that forces us to speak
                          when we should be silent.

Our first city was the Tower of Babel
Noah's descendants built to reach heaven.
But the ancient gods confounded their ambitions
and turned their language into babble till they
no longer understood one another or the world.
Stone by stone and log by beam we have built
city after city, tied studs and joists and braces
into frames, placed brick on brick, dug moats
and sewers, poured concrete, laid out streets
and squares—only to sack burn raze bomb
and level them again because who dwell
in them no longer hear each other in the din
babble and hubbub of their own making.
And still we are building cities though the gods
have long abandoned us, and the cities grow
larger and their destruction more spectacular,
more woeful. Ordinary citizens never found
the safety they sought in their homes that were
their castles only for those whose homes were
castles to begin with and even they had to design
squeaks into their floorboards to foil assassins.
How to guide the ordinary in the ways
of *kami*—the extraordinary that we are?

                         Prince Shōtoku laboured for a whole generation
                           to frame a constitution that could house a nation
                              in the way of Buddha, and the sun and the moon
                                did not lose their brightness when he died,
                                 nor did heaven and earth crumble to ruin
                               as his people feared. He left behind the blueprint

for a state of harmony and moved on to the next
stage in the cycle of his dying and being
time and again in this blind world of pain
until he might find through enlightenment escape
to a peace absolute in its moveless nothingness.

If it can be said
It cannot be true only
A koan can hint
At the truth that nothing is
Everything is in Mu.

America is energy, not contemplation,
and Manhattan harbours no humility.
It feeds on the illusions Hollywood
manufactures that life is a movie
to be scripted and directed: Action!
Cut! Action for the hero
to punch his way to happiness.
The makers of the bomb aimed
to punch the enemy into submission
even if it meant blowing up
a couple of hundred thousand
women and children—*Orientals*,
said Rabi, chief advisor to
the Manhattan Project, *are not people
one loves...I think with my hands.*

And with their hands they spread death
from the skies. Bohr and Fermi opposed
the bomb they made, demanded a demo
in the desert for all the world to witness
the horror as a warning to make peace.
FDR agreed and died, leaving Harry
to give the green light to General Groves,
the obese bully in charge of delivering
the goods, and he was gung ho
to drop the bomb on Kyoto to achieve
maximum casualties and shock, to say
nothing of the publicity value of obliterating
three thousand shrines and temples,

a center of learning, a chunk of history.
Luck and the weather saved Kyoto
and sentenced Hiroshima to death.

I walked the path of philosophy between temples
and along a gentle stream in Kyoto, strolled
under the filigree canopy of its colonnades
of cherry trees, leafless in March. A chill wind
was blowing snowflakes like a blizzard of blossoms
through them. It starts at the Inn of the White Sand—
Hashimoto's house filled with poetry and paintings,
Greek pottery, Persian miniatures, and he made
his garden a composition in rock and plant,
tree, sculpture, and their reflections in the pond
through which ponderous koi glide too ancient
for the gaudy colours lavished on them.
Among stone lanterns, iris, lotus flowers, and
trained pines buddhas meditate in bamboo stands
across the centuries. The mind is wedded here
to nature as a boat sailing is to wind and sea.
Into a rock hauled from Kurama on a cart
drawn by four oxen a Chinese hand has chiseled
the characters that inspired Hashimoto,
the painter, as they sustain all civilization:
The Spirit of Art must be Free!

        Across the seeker's path the shōgun Ashikaga
        built his silver mansion to indulge his passion
        for the moon, for women and tea ceremonies,
    which drained him of his silver—except for the sea
        of sand whose furrows were sculptured
        in his sumptuous garden to ripple the silver
        moonlight and pattern the night around
        Kagetsudai—the image of Mt. Fuji.
        He left Ginkaku to the monks for a temple
        where in black lacquered spaces Kan non,
    the goddess of mercy, now dwells with a thousand
        statues of Jizo, the guardian god of children.
        If they protected the children of Kyoto it was
        at the price of Hiroshima's and Nagasaki's:

Shiguru's incinerated body was identified
from the lunch box he was still clutching;
Moto's charred body tagged
by one lens and one temple of her glasses
melted to her cheek bones;
they recognized Kozo's burnt body only
from the remnants of his boots;
only the buckle of the belt on Takashi's
school uniform survived;
and Yoshika's body was never found,
only her burnt water bottle—
school girls and school boys, all of them, thousands
of them wasted to a triumph of science and politics.

This is the month Blake died
who beheld the universe in a grain
of sand and innocence in a child's
eye, and Conrad who journeyed
into the dark recesses of the human
heart, and Mann who examined
the pact ambition makes with
Mephistopheles, and Balzac who saw
through the human tragicomedy—
they understood that who seeks
knowledge in pursuit of power
comes upon wisdom like a wasp
flying into a spider net: he destroys
it or he will be destroyed by it.
The soft voice of the visionary
goes unheeded in the din of demagogues.
The path to the lighthouse is perilous:
it leads across cliffs at the mercy
of wind and surf to where the keeper
must hold solitary vigil
and send signals into the night
not knowing who receives them—

or else the fate of nations
is left to the blind and the deaf,
the professional self-servers,
whether blatant or sophisticated:

the academic and the military,
Oppenheimer and Groves,
the genius and the general,
the urbane and the vulgar,
chain smoker and teetotaler—
an odd couple joined
by pride and hubris
in a devious scheme.
Ignore the signals the mind
sends and we are left
to inflict on each other
the violence of the universe
in the tiny spacetime
left us for a greater ecstasy.

The sun is a nuclear holocaust born from a cloud
of dust that extended beyond the most distant planet
and floated in a void until a shock wave from another
distant star exploding set it in slow motion rotating
faster and faster collapsing for 10 million years
till it ignited at the center and our star lit up
an infrared cocoon where other vortexes of dust
were rotating collapsing sweeping up the skies
spheres too small to start their own fires
fated by chance to be satellites forever of the giant
sun whose body can accommodate a million earths
and whose energies hold the planets in their orbits
determine their lives, our lives. The light that now thrusts
the magenta of a bull thistle's flower into my eyes
was generated at the sun's core before the last ice age,
before the Gravettians and the wooly mammoths,
about the time the last Neanderthaler died in France.
Temperatures around 15 million degrees still
accelerate protons in the sun's core to collide
100 million times a second with enough force
eventually after rebounding septillion times each
to override their refusal to fuse and surrender
the energy that must travel thirty millennia
to reach the sun's surface which is no surface
and has no surface for a body would fall through its fire
faster than through air if it were not instantly vaporized.

Sunlight behind leaves
Luminous green on sky blue
Wind shifting colours
Gestures on a human scale
Best measure infinity.

Shōtoku's 17 articles brought the great change
for which Kamatari and Naka-no-ōe built
a city that was to be the center of an empire
where social harmony was to shine like a sun
upon rulers and ruled alike: Nara—
city of timbered temples like music carved
into wood where I walked the path
of history to the Buddha's sublime smile.
A blind priest struggled from China to deliver
his message to the emperor and Shoma
ordered Tōdajii to be built with two pagodas
300 ft tall and the world's greatest hall
to be raised in wood there to be cast
in bronze serenity and peace large enough
to fill the heart of his people. Though
the magic of its gilt *kutsugata* at the corners
of the roof could not fend off the evils of fire
the Daibutsuden endures, its massive beams
darkened with age and incense. In the gentle
geometry of Nara the ways of the gods
converged with wisdom under the lotus tree
in compassion, and a temple to commemorate
the birth of a nation stands as a halfway house
for the weary on their arduous road to the future.

Is this the story
of the President's beasts
and the unlovables
of atomic physicists
and trigger-happy
generals? Or is theirs
the view through the tight
ass of pride?
Were the pilgrims
who landed at Plymouth

to build the City of God
bound to leave
so many wastelands
at home and abroad?
When power is
wedded to faith
worlds founder
in thunder and lightning.
There is something
in the logic of unreason
that turns the heart
to stone. Even Einstein
supported the bomb
and lived to regret it
seeing *the drift towards*
unparalleled catastrophe.
Blindness is a condition
of those (but not only of those)
who bow their heads before
the charlatans of ideology
instead of birdflight and waterfall:
they turn into terrorists
because they feed their spirits
stridency and starve it
of the silence of trees
staunchly climbing mountains.

It took 500 flying fortresses and two night raids
on Tokyo by order of General LeMay
to turn streets into rivers of fire
and people into burning matchsticks.
Some of the crews in the B-29s vomited
from the stench of burning flesh filling
the heavens: more than 100,000 civilians
roasted and a million homes torched.
But General Groves determined to out-do
his rivals, out-destroy out-kill
with the mother of all bombs:
one plane one bomb one flash—
neat and simple as a Nazi slogan:
ein Volk ein Reich ein Führer!
Only the dying was more complex
more furtive more lingering.

This blood century's first great war too
was waiting, like all wars, in a world
of privilege and poverty to happen.
It needed only the crook of a finger
in Sarajevo to trigger the looping of pride
and fear back and forth between Vienna
and Belgrade, Berlin and London,
Moscow and Paris, feeding the equations
of greed and hatred back again and again
into the diplomatic chaos until the fractals
of war began to emerge in patterns
of blood—a beauty too terrible for words.
This is the month the first World War
started as the misguided masses of Europe
answered the call *pro patria deoque*
and began the long march to fifty million
soldiers' graves that ended at Versailles
with the signatures of revenge to a treaty
that guaranteed and delivered another war.

If it is true that he
who kills moth or butterfly
shall never be loved
by man or woman,
what is to become of those
whose riches and reputations
were made by the bomb,
by any bomb or bullet—
what is to become of them,
of us all?

Up in that blue and tranquil sky
serene as Buddha's smile
then as now here and there
the Enola Gay is over its target
on Special Mission No.13
and its crew become characters
in a twentieth century Noh play
performing a ritual murder
too stilted for their true emotions:

Pilot: *We're about to start*
the bomb run.
Put on your goggles.

Bombardier: *I've got it.—*
Bomb away!.....
See anything yet?

Tail Gunner: *No, sir...* (forty seconds later)
Yes, sir!!!
A huge circular cloud
as if a ring around some distant
planet has detached itself
and is coming up
toward us!

A thunderous shock wave shakes the plane
and lifts it violently up towards the sun.

Pilot: *Flak!!!*

Tail Gunner: *There's another one coming!*

Another shock wave.
Another surge toward the sun.

Pilot: *OK. That was the reflected*
shock wave. There won't be
any more. Stay calm.

Tail Gunner: *A column of smoke is rising fast...*
It has a fiery core... Fires
are springing up everywhere...
There are too many to count...
Here it comes—
the mushroom shape...

Pilot: *Target visually bombed*
with good results.

Weaponeer: *Good? Hell—*
results clear-cut.
Successful in all respects.
Visual effects greater than
Alamogordo!

Pilot: *The destruction is bigger*
than I had really imagined.

Co-pilot: *My God, what have we done?*

Hiroshima: city and port
spread between two ranges of hills
like an open fan
across the delta of the river Ōta
transformed into an inferno
at exactly 8:16 a.m.
August 6, 1945:
first the flash the pika
then the blue whitehot blaze
          that few survived who saw it
then the blast the shock wave
          that perforated human bodies
          even miles away with splinters
          of glass wood stone metal
          like shrapnell
and then the heat wave
          igniting a firestorm
          that raged across the ruins
          two hours later at 65 km/h
          and consumed what was left
          of buildings and survivors
          too slow to escape—
waves, circles more deadly
than Dante's hell, rings of destruction:
in a radius of 1 km from ground zero
90% of all living beings killed instantly,
in a radius of 2 km
all buildings destroyed,
in a radius of 3 km
heat rays caused primary burns—

a circle 10 km across left to chaos
a city wasted a desert of rubble
without light or water or food
a hundred thousand children women men
dead or dying that first day
and perhaps as many to die
in the weeks months years to follow
from a disease born like a bolt from heaven
that catastrophic day—radiation sickness:
in the smouldering of the 125-bed
Communications Hospital 2,500 victims
crammed into corridors stairways toilets
without doors or windows with festering
wounds and raw burns vomiting urinating
defecating blood wherever they lay
on filthy tatamis without help or hope
for less than 10% of doctors and nurses
in the city survived the first impact
and they couldn't diagnose the sickness
they had never known or heard of
and they couldn't treat anyone
for there were no medical supplies:
no bandages, no antiseptics, no painkillers...

> My God, what have we done!
> Surely if I can hear the groans and cries
> across half a century and around half the globe
> someone in the ubiquitous order of angels
> should've listened and heard. Instead
> the blue morning mushroomed into a dark
> and noxious cloud from which black rain fell
> and streaked broken walls and stunted trees,
> black raindrops settling on the dying dead
> and living, staining the pure pink of children's
> raw flesh—heaven's answer to their pleas.

Here the morning is a blue scrim
across the sky hiding the stars
and the vast indifferent void between them
only from the truly blind. The storms
of war and youth have long dispersed

the airy angels of my childhood.
Life flickers fragile between nuclear
holocausts and the cosmic deepfreeze
that turns blood to stone.

> How is it men who have mastered
> the mathematics of Armageddon
> cannot put two and two together
> on a sunny August morning?

> The sun's light deceives
> Those who seek solace in space
> Night rules absolute
> Dawn is but a wake-up call
> To find the light inside you.

Did the Empress Shōtoku see the light
in her love for a Buddhist priest
and did Dōkyō see it in his lust for power
that led them to disgrace and murder foul?
Who can look into the seeds of time
and say which will grow and which die?
The seeds of art and music drifted across
the seas from China and took root:
the dulcet song of the five-stringed lute
inlaid with tortoise shell and agate,
carved and coloured masks to dramatize
the dance, the swift and gentle firmness
of the brush on the scroll conjuring
mountains, flowers and the wisdom of sages:

> In the wind's eddies
> Cherry blossoms rock and whirl
> Their sweet scent wafted
> High on invisible waves
> To ebb away in the sky.

The eight-armed Buddha with a lotus flower
holds out a rope to climb to enlightenment,
a black pearl in his forehead—a third eye:
can it see the future in the seed?

35

The Sutra of the Golden Light promises
peace and prosperity to all nations
on the path of charity and compassion
where meanness is erased from the heart.
Imagine light where there is no darkness
and listen to the 4,500 poems of the Manyōshū
sing of sun and moon, rivers, trees, the seasons
of the heart: sorrow yearning love.

And so tradition weaves the centuries together.
The Emperor Kammu moved his court to Kyoto
and put the Fujiwara clan on the throne
for two centuries. Another city was born
whose winging temple roofs forever lift
the mind beyond the raging stars. Men
rehearsed the rules of government and worship
while women tended to the native tongue
recording the memories on which tradition
feeds: court ladies in love with the cuckoo's
call at dawn and anything that cries at night
(except babies), indulging pen and brush
in diaries and pillow books exulting
in the splendour and privilege of their class
which men defined and defended with sword
and statute for the greater benefit of all
who benefited. And Murasaki telling the tale
of Prince Genji's adventures: a woman creating
a universe of emotions in which a man travels
from knowledge of woman to a quest for truth—
never-ending journey of the wondering mind.

A millennium later men who never
travelled anywhere but to display
the void at their core strut
across the world stage playing
buffoons and barbarians
with such aplomb to make
this century a season of blood,
its equinox a sunny August morning
at the hour of the dog
when they made of Hiroshima
the epitome of their own hell:

After the *pikadon* the procession of corpses
survivors picking their way among ruins
burning houses tangles of torn cables
and wires charred shrunken bodies rubble—
slow march of barely human shapes clothes
blasted or burnt off moving as in a nightmare
numb with shock and pain moaning crying
driven by instinct to escape they know not what
the fire the smoke the dust the horror they can't
comprehend women men children flayed alive
their skin hanging in strips from what is left
of their faces their torsos walking zombies
hair torched frizzled shuffling bewildered
schoolgirls their pigtails burnt to crisp stiff horns
holding their arms away from the raw flesh
bleeding blistering some without faces
ears noses lips melted by the fire you can't
tell the back of the head from the front
if it weren't for the moaning: *mizu...mizu...mizu...*—
But there is no water to put out the fires
inside them or outside on their skins in the streets.

Bashō's frog leapt into the pond
with a splash that can be heard still
and will be heard for as long as
there are knowing ears—like the *pikadon*
that changed the world forever and
the bang at the birth of the universe
that fills the void still with a hum.
The seeker's mind hears the inaudible.

Voices bite into this morning's
blue serenity. Sound bytes
from hell. Replayed over and over.
Mizu...mizu...eraiyo...eraiyo...—
I cannot bear the pain.
The sun has climbed into the treetops
yet it is still 8:16 a.m.: the flash
the blast the firestorm—then the parade
of whimpering skeletons. Time
stands still where there is no hope.

It is still August 6, 1945
and we have used the half-century since
to stockpile enough nuclear bombs
to fry every city and every citizen
on this planet to a crisp. The tiny pink
flowers of pokeweed have brought forth
poisonous black berries whose carmine
juice yields a dye to paint blood
all over nature's blue-green canvas.

Look at your image
In the mirror is clouded
Beauty you can paint
Only when you break your brush
And draw it with empty hands.

Force and matter are both
a matter of particles. Yet
a jackpine cannot occupy
the space of a birch. Trees
don't add up, nor do flowers
or people—but their force
does. Mysteriously
their integral spin unites
bosons to make forests
burn hotter and brighter
than a match and the larger
earth holds back the sea
against the moon's pull.
The half integral spin
of fermions condemns
all that exists in bodies
to compete for a place
in the endless cosmic night.

The gardens of Japan transform force
into elegance embodying the asymmetry
of the universe in designs so intricately simple
stream and flower, rock and tree are joined
in music to inspire Heinan nobles to float
poems on lily-padded ponds as they sip

tea or sake translating passion into decorum.
There is a way to throw a spear with hands
empty, but the Taira and Minamoto warriors
never learnt the art. In bloody disturbances
they took by sword what the pen had
turned into song. Emperors retired to their palace
gardens and ruled for seven hundred years
by counsel and intrigue while shōguns with iron
hand and implacable minds ran the affairs of state.
Between Kamakura and Tokugawa samurai
enforced peace so that the soft strings
of the kōto could learn to ease sorrow
and heighten joy and the thirty-one syllables
of the tanka could capture the seasons:

> Pink blossoms in spring
> In summer the green ricefields
> Autumn's ginkgo gold
> And the snowdrifts of winter
> Painted with a brush of fire.

> By bloodshed Yorimoto created order
> and settled on the archipelago the virtue
> of justice. The gods sent a typhoon
> in August—a *kamikaze* to destroy
> Kublai Khan's fleet, drown his army,
> and save the people of the rising sun
> from Mongol slaughter or slavery.
> Yoshimitzu built a golden pavillion
> between heaven and earth—
> a glittering jewel reflecting shōgun
> refinement in the koi-furrowed lake.

Thus civilization travelled by boat,
on horse-back, by the wise pen
and the bloody sword. The affairs
of men and women have their seasons
too. Harvests of song and dance
alternate with slaughter in battle,
the meditations of the *shakuhachi* flute
give way to the groans of war's victims

till Nobunaga defeated his *damyo* rivals
and set fire to a mountain to rid himself
of Kyoto's meddlesome monks: he killed
tens of thousands of them, their women
and children, then built a tall castle
of stone and wood with moats
and ramparts to withstand the new
weapon: cannons. A Tokugawa tower rose
to guard the sky and the peace that turned
the nation into a strict and exclusive
but caring family functional for three
centuries. Samurai became civil servants
and moved to Edo, a fishing village growing
into a metropolis where Kabuki actors
to the twang of the three-stringed *samisen*
flute, clappers and drums entertained
riotously with tales of star-crossed lovers
come to grief between passion and propriety—
the age-old rocks of tragedy for every
wand'ring bark. Bashō extracted serene
melancholy from the passage of all things
through the season's filter of images pressed
into the haiku's tight vat. Poets sang and
painters spread life and times across scrolls
of silk and paper as writers plotted between
romance, satire and melodrama, mask,
pantomime and suspense the never-ending
human comedy of fancies and follies.

It was the merchants forced the last shōgun
to resign and Emperor Meiji to throw open
the gates to the Western world shut tight
for centuries. And they came from beyond
the seas with machines and money to haul
these islands into another age—the industrial
the technological, the nuclear age!

The wind and the leaves
Clouds condensing in the air
Fish parting the waves
My hand fondling your hair—all
Exchanges of energy.

Matter and energy are two sides of the same embrace.
The universe may be a tiny bubble of spacetime
sprung from the void and blown out of all proportions
and we are inside it, circumscribed by its infinite finity
and a mind that can no more comprehend its own
workings than a grape can come to taste its own wine.
Let us drink to the forces that have filtered
through space from chaos a moment
for us to invest with beauty and truth.

The light which paints the morning
landscape across my window and
the warmth that caresses your face
are the remnants of a nuclear holocaust
tamed on its 8½ minute ride to earth;
they were born in a cauldron that burns
700 million tons of hydrogen a second
to fend off the force of gravity
which will some day crush
and leave the sun a black dwarf.
The universe happens
between vast voids by violence,
created on a scale of numbers
that never add up to anything
comprehensible and leave us nothing
but a speck of time and space
to defy it with a gesture of gentleness—
a moment of music, circles of dance
and embrace, unknown
in the brutal gyrations of stars.
So fragile the window for the mind
to reach and wonder, to open
the door a crack and hold its hand
into the mystery and feel something
passing in the dark.

Bunraku puppets
Beethoven's *Grosse Fuge*
The Sistine Chapel—
Voices to touch and move us
Beyond the known and measured.

Goldfinches flit among the flowers of the Yellow
Goat's Beard whose seedfaces are open now
and follow the sun until noon. Across Ontario
children on their vacations are leaping into lakes
and rivers or fishing from boats with their fathers
trawling casting angling while their mothers tan
by the dock. Breakfast is over and life is good.
Countless snapshots will be taken today,
August 6, to hold fast at least 1/100 second
of a smile, of shared sunshine joy and peace.
Where to put these photos in the albums
of so many summers in so many places?

A ten-year-old bent over
the burnt and blistered body
of his dead little sister
crying: *Mako! Mako!*
Please don't die!

A woman naked raw
pink as fried octopus
a charred infant still
attached to her nipple
scrawling her name on a wall
with her own blood because
her lips are burnt beyond speech.

A man (perhaps) grotesquely
scorched without nose or ears
drinking black blood-stained
vomit water from a reservoir
filled with people boiled alive.

Give me back my mother
give me back my father
give me back my childhood
give me back myself...

The President sent *very warm congratulations*
to the General on the success of the A-bomb:
This is the greatest day in history!
and all the President's men cheered.

Twelve-year-old Susumu—No no!
Don't look at her blistered face
so swollen she is blind and mute.
Instead, look at the river—No no no!!
Don't look at the river log-jammed
with bodies...men children women
who leapt into the current to cool
their burning skin their bleeding
perforated limbs and bled to death
or drowned...corpses floating in
spilled oil blood filth debris...lovers
embracing in death...fathers mothers
trying to save daughters sons
their parents siblings husbands...—
No no no no—don't look!!!
Don't listen to the groaning
whimpering crying...*mizu mizu*...
In the metropolis of water...*eraiyo
eraiyo*...—Stop up your ears!
You must take leave of your senses
or you'll smell the sweet fishy stench
of burning human flesh. Sore and dazed
survivors are already lighting makeshift
pyres built from the wreckage of their
homes to burn their dead loved ones.
Acrid fumes sting your eyes. Close them!
Or you'll see the flying ashes take wing
swarms of black flies laying eggs
in raw wounds that'll soon squirm
with nests of maggots.—No. Don't look!
For there are no ointments no bandages
no doctors...no no no—don't listen!
Victors never listen never see never
speak except of their victory. Be one
of them—the three Chinese monkeys!

Thirteen years and a few hundred thousand
victims later Harry wrote the city fathers
of Hiroshima he would do it all over again.
And all the scientists clapped and cheered
Oppie who gave them the boxer's victory salute.

The General was so proud and pleased he rushed
to drop *Fat Man* on Nagasaki three days later
for a repeat performance of the *pikadon*:
the flash the blast the firestorm—
lest the Japs spoil his triumph and surrender.
And a Talmudic student from a village
in Lithuania came to America, changed
his name to William (the Bard) Leonardo
(the Genius) Laurence (his street), exchanged
Jahweh for Mammon and Mephistopheles:
I am destiny, he wrote in the cockpit of Bock's Car
over Nagasaki as he looked down on *the thousands
of little children who certainly had nothing
to do with the war...They were like a fatted calf,
you know, saved for the slaughter. I know
they don't know...that this is their last night
on earth*. And Bill exulted—for a fee
he had become the bomb's official panegyrist,
America's nuclear cheer-leader: *Prometheus
brought a new fire down to earth.*

　　　　　I'd like to fly over there, wrote the mother
　　　of a GI killed in action in the Pacific, *and drop
　　　more bombs myself.* Grief can be deadly.
　　　And she knew nothing of the legions
　　　of comfort women raped a thousand times
　　　a day from Korea to the Philippines by Asia's
　　　master race. Or of the Bataan death march
　　　of US and Filipino POWs starved and beaten
　　　to death by their captors. Or of the victorious
　　　soldiers who bayonetted pregnant women
　　　in China before roasting them by the pound
　　　on a spit for supper. *When you deal with beasts
　　　you have to treat them as beasts. This is
　　　the happiest day of my life.*

　　　　　　　　Don't listen to their words,
　　　　　　　my weary reader, they know not
　　　　　　　what they say. They cannot be
　　　　　　　what they say. Words streak across
　　　　　　　the mind's night sky like meteors,

their core fragments of memories
burning with shame and desire
fear and pity, dimly lighting up
the shadows of shapes and figures
distorted in time's concave optic
and through the convex lenses
of tears. There are tears in all things,
even in the Buddha's smile
for only their passing is eternal.

This is the month Ghengis Khan died
whose hordes conquered Asia
by murder and rape, exterminating
the kingdoms of Xia Xia, Ogodai, Kublai,
spreading a sea of blood across
the mountains of China and Russia's plains
unmatched in seven centuries until the killing
fields of Flanders, Cambodia, and Vietnam,
the holocausts in Germany, Russia, China,
the butcheries in Bosnia, Chile, El Salvador,
Indonesia, Guatemala, and Rwanda,
the horrors of Dresden and Hiroshima.

Who will break the killing cycle?
Beasts have long ritualized their anger.
They know the future of the fittest
is a function of the fellowship of all.
But we feed on the illusion that each
human is an island unto himself
each independent and superior.
And so our B-29s rain burning oil
and napalm on cities built of bamboo,
wood, and rice paper to turn them
into fields of fire, ashes and tears.
Where the winds and waves of strife
disrupt peace and even the gods preach
revenge, spring and summer fall and
winter turn into seasons of blood.

Don't look back at the ruins of this city
at the foot of the scorched hills of Ushima

45

under the mushroom cloud, this Pompeii
man-made that preserved not even the agony
of the bodies, only a few shadows—
a human shape standing on a ladder
radiation-seared into concrete, the outline
of a child surprised in the act of being
alive. Don't look back for a black
and gritty rain is coating what is left
of Hiroshima, its dead and its dying,
with a scourge more malignant and terminal
than the plague—a slow tortuous breakdown
in the blood: first petechiae, purple spots
on the skin, then ulcerating gums, mouths,
bloody vomit and diarrhea, fever, anorexia
and oh—the pain the fatigue the despair!
Later more severe internal hemorrhaging,
purpura, finally epilation, total loss of hair—
a halo of death around the grey heads
of children, women, men. For weeks
they perished, for months, thousands.
Years later the bomb was still picking
its victims, even among the unborn.

Cry not for the dead
but for the living. The man
who played the violin
pleaded for the bomb.
When convictions replace
comprehension the hand
that writes poetry
will pull the trigger.
In the thickets of our heart
flowers as beautiful
as lovers and poisonous
as the Destroying Angel
of our woodlands, grow
to monstrous size and shapes
only to perish with us.
A black void spat us
into this blinding light
to wander in a cloud

of unknowing the opposites
that'll cancel each other
and us when we no longer
endure and celebrate them.
Our days are no more
dependable than our nights.
The stars deny our existence
and afford us neither moral
high-ground nor reality checks.
We are what we become
on our solitary travels
from one darkness to another
learning to clap
with one hand applauding
what is beyond our reach
while the other reaches
far beyond its grasp.

I walked the path of peace in Hiroshima
from the coloured neon ads of its downtown
shopping streets reconstructed in the image
of those who destroyed them, past the hysteric
clinking of *pachinko* parlours where the greed
that fuels war makes the poor poorer
and the rich richer, just like wars. You have to
leave them far behind to reach the park of peace
where the bomb's victims have come to rest
in a mound of ashes under charred disfigured
trees in the shadow of the skeletal dome of
technology. An old man on a cane, his face
scarred by fire, his ears burnt off, shuffled
to the cenotaph, dropped a bunch of flowers,
silently, furtively, as he had done, rain or sun,
wind or snow, every day for half a century
because he cannot, will not, forget,
and he is still dying, his heart still singing:

> *Give me back my mother*
> *give me back my father*
> *give me back my sons and daughters*
> *give me back myself.*

What are the triumphs of science
if they but unleash suffering?
They can only measure the distance
we have travelled from harmony
to hubris. We are destined to search
for a light to chart a course
through this darkness. A single candle
in the heart is worth a billion supernovae
on the other side of the universe.
We are born to hold a candle to the mind
and name the unnameable. No one
will ever see a quark or a black hole:
their mystery is a matter of mathematics.
But the green leaves that'll soon colour
fall are not a formula, nor is the wind
in your hair. Solitary wanderers
whom the light of love shows the way
home, in our embrace we know
the illusions of touch and taste image
scent and song are our real world.

Some mornings never pass
but the earth moves on
spinning us between cosmic fires
through all the seasons of our days,
the years, the aeons in a calendar
calculated well beyond our ken.
The sun has reached its zenith now,
its glare intense enough to buckle
even crack the striae in stones.
The heat is heavy with the weight
of vaporized clouds. The birds
have fallen silent in the trees
sweating in their own shadows.
The land is wearying of the sun
and longs for a season of respite.
Wintergreen shelters its white
and waxy flowers close to the ground
like urns in the axil of its leaves,
harbouring the aroma of succulent
berries redder and sweeter than blood.

A groundhog is feasting in the garden
in anticipation of a long cold sleep.
All is energy. We have yet to provide
for the mind's never-ending quest.

Adako was two years old
when black rain fell on her
in Hiroshima. Ten years later
she fainted in her schoolyard.
Leukemia. Though she folded
9,964 paper cranes
the bomb's radioactive tentacles
took her, 36 cranes short
of longevity. Will science
achieve that too?

Tell the samurai of the world death
is heavier than a mountain when fools
think duty is a feather in their cap.
Today those who grieve are floating paper
boats with burning candles down the Ōta river
to carry the names of the bomb's victims
down to the forgiving sea. But their blood
won't be washed off this century's history.

Tonight I shall go to the city and
in the setting sun leap into the stream
of faces—faces never black or white
but in myriad shades of dusk and dawn,
olive, rosé, brown, grey and ivory—
bobbing adrift on a tide of the world's
unseen and unwept tears past restaurants
and stores, offices, churches and homes, built
from their passion for peace and happiness.
I shall slip through the curtain of their eyes
to browse in their hearts among all the world's
tales of fear and pity, folly and greed
in search of the force that in the starry night
lights a Buddha's smile and powers the future.

A hawk floats past noon
on the sky's blue waters
in circles drifting slowly
across the golden light.
Its shadow passes over
this green summer's day
like the hand of a ghost.

Afterword by the Author

Across the Sun's Warp is the sixth poem in a cycle which represents a quest for an understanding of the point humanity has reached today in its turbulent development as the dominating species on this planet. While each poem has a separate identity that does not require knowledge of the others for an understanding, the poems are at the same time interrelated by imagery, tone, and plot, and it is therefore useful at least to be aware that the complete cycle is now intended to consist of twelve poems, one for each month of the year, subdivided in groups of three to represent the four seasons, and is entitled *Seasons of Blood*.

The first section encompasses *The Ides of March*, *April Fools*, and *May Song and Dance*. It was published in 1984 by Mosaic Press under the title *Season of Blood*. I now wish I had published it by its subtitle, *Spring: Bloodroot*, but I had no idea at the time that I had embarked upon a journey in poetry that would last the rest of my life. The structure as well as the objective of the poem unfolded only in the process of writing it, a process that is still ongoing. *Across the Sun's Warp*, the most recently completed, is the third poem in the second section, *Summer: The Devil's Club*, whose preceding two poems are called *Where Shall the Birds Fly?* and *When Africa Calls Uhuru*.

While the focus of *Seasons of Blood* is that bloodiest of centuries, the twentieth, the poems travel back in time as far as imagination will carry them. The objective seems to be to discover how we have come to this point in our history, with a view to possibly casting some light on a viable path into the future at a time when all such paths seem to lead into an increasingly ominous darkness. All of which may simply be a way of asking the question: Who are we? The poems seek not answers as much as imaginative ways of raising and refining the questions.

The strategy involves four dimensions: the order of nature (to which we belong), politics/history (what we have made of nature), the new sciences (how we understand that order today), and the human mind embedded in this matrix and yet rising above it. Specifically, nature is embodied in the flora and fauna of southeastern Ontario from where the poet embarks on his journeys which take him to different times and different countries across the world. The choice of the country is, in part, determined by significant historical events in the twentieth century associated with the month in which the poem is set.

Across the Sun's Warp represents August in the cycle, and takes us to Japan because August 6, 1945, marks the first use of an atomic bomb (dropped by the U.S. on Hiroshima), a turning point in human history.

The global geography of **Seasons of Blood** is not only a consequence of the poem's universal concerns, but also a product of its being written in Canada whose streets are crowded with the histories of all the world's peoples in the flesh. Their story is our story, and this is how it must be told.

Ayorama, May 21, 2003